THE **MOST** PREDICTABLE **WAY** TO GET RICH

THE **MOST** PREDICTABLE **WAY** TO GET RICH

ROBERT ELDER

FEATURING ROBERT ELDER AND OTHER LEADING REAL ESTATE EXPERTS

The Most Predictable Way to Get Rich

Published by Millionaire Investment Club

ISBN: 9781984234049

Printed in Canada

THE **MOST** PREDICTABLE WAY TO GET RICH

INTRODUCTION

IF YOU'RE READING THIS BOOK, it's safe to say that you are thinking about learning to invest in real estate. Maybe you're disappointed in what your current investments are doing. The stock market is making a lot of people nervous lately, and that isn't doing anyone's retirement account any favors. Maybe you're looking for a new career, and you heard this might be an exciting way to make loads of money. Maybe you're not sure why you're interested, but someone said that you should find out what investing in real estate can do for you.

I get questions all the time from people who want to know how I did it. Then they want to know how THEY can do this - they want to know which area or investment niche they should focus on, and they *really* want to know how to fit all this into their current lifestyle. I can tell you not only MY story, but I found nine other colleagues who were willing to share THEIR stories to help you get started.

You'll find it all here - inspiration, focus, goal-setting, brainstorming, motivation - everything you need to begin the next great phase of your life. You'll find out how to know which investment style or strategy suits your personality, your goals, and the lifestyle you hope to have as a real estate

investor. You'll learn what it takes to make your ideal strategy work for you. By the end of the book, you will hopefully be able to see yourself as not just a successful investor, but a successful person.

Real estate can provide you with a lifestyle and freedom beyond your wildest dreams. The only thing holding you back is really *you*! You have the power to change your preconceived notions of why this wouldn't work for you. You have the power to overcome your own self-limiting beliefs. And *only you* have the power to allow the information in this book to make a difference in your life. Most of the experts in this book started with little or nothing but the courage to take that first leap, and they have accumulated wealth, success, and freedom from a J-O-B.

Go ahead. Read on, and learn how you can make all this a part of your life, too. It may be the most life-changing decision you ever make!

In 37 years as a landlord, ROBERT *ELDER has owned houses, duplexes, apartment complexes, office and industrial buildings, and a hotel. Starting from scratch, he has built a present portfolio of over 600 unites and properties. Robert shares this experience with other investors through trainings at:*

MILLIONAIRE POSSIBILITIES – A LANDLORD AND PROPERTY INVESTORS ASSOCIATION with monthly meetings in Oklahoma City, OK, and online at MPmeeting.com. MP members have used techniques and action items to launch real estate careers and create millions in profits.

Millionaire Real Estate Club, REAL ESTATE COACHING AND LEGAL CONSULTING, where Robert personally works with experienced investors committed to outrageous success in their own business ventures.

Robert holds degrees in Finance, Economics, and Math, along with an MBA in Accounting and a Juris Doctorate. He is a licensed attorney in Oklahoma.

If you have any questions for Robert, you can contact him at:

Complete Home Rentals

8801 N. Western Avenue

Oklahoma City, OK 73114

(405) 286-2000

Robert@millionairerealestateclub.com

CHAPTER ONE

HOW THE FEDERAL GOVERNMENT HELPED ME TO BECOME A REAL ESTATE MILLIONAIRE

THE FEDERAL GOVERNMENT PAYS ME about $2 million per year in rent for my rental properties. You can do exactly the same thing, on any scale you wish - even with as little as one rental house.

My real estate story began when I was a teenager. Donald Trump has said that greed is good, and as a young man I certainly experienced an element of greed.

One of the very first things I wanted was a Jaguar XKE, a beautiful sports car. I could picture myself driving that beautiful car, talking on my satellite telephone, and - most importantly - experiencing complete freedom. I wanted the ability to do what I wanted to do when I wanted to do it, and go where I wanted to go whenever I wanted to go there.

I knew that to do this, I would need to own my own business. I didn't call it passive income back then but, I knew that I would want income that came to me regularly even if I wasn't working. I decided that I would need to be a millionaire, but I had no clue how to become one. I didn't grow up in a rich family. I didn't know anybody who was rich. I didn't even know anyone who was successful in owning their own business or being self-employed.

As I thought about how I might become a millionaire, I explored different businesses and different investments, and I came to a simple and profound conclusion. The most predictable way for me to become a millionaire was to buy and hold rental houses.

I'm even more convinced today that this was not only the most predictable way for me to become a millionaire, but it is also the most predictable way for YOU to become a millionaire.

THE FIVE WEALTH SECRETS ALL REAL ESTATE MILLIONAIRES KNOW AND USE

As I thought about using real estate as a tool to help me become a millionaire, the first secret that came to me was that I could use Other People's Money (OPM). I could use OPM to fund of the bulk of each real estate purchase. This simply means that I would borrow most of the purchase price.

Not only that, but since I would make the payments out of the money that I received as rent, I would be using OPM to make the monthly mortgage payments, and once the mortgage had been paid off in full, I would own the

property free and clear. That's how I discovered the first of the five wealth secrets.

WEALTH SECRET #1: OTHER PEOPLE'S MONEY

You can use OPM to purchase rental real estate, and you can use OPM to pay off the mortgage. For example, if you find a $50,000 house and you put 10 percent ($5,000) down, you will finance the remaining 90 percent of the purchase price ($45,000) with OPM.

In the table below, there is an example of how this works with a $ 45,000 mortgage. The mortgage balance column is the mortgage balance at the end of each year. This is also known as the currant balance or the principal.

Notice that the amount due on the principal decreases by a greater amount as the years go by. This is because the lower the principal gets, the less interest it charges, so more of your mortgage payment can go to reduce the balance due on the amount you originally borrowed.

Year	Mortgage Balance	Year	Mortgage Balance	Year	Mortgage Balance
1	$ 43,091	6	$ 31,628	11	$ 16,167
2	$ 41,064	7	$ 28,895	12	$ 12,479
3	$ 38,913	8	$ 25,992	13	$ 8,565
4	$ 36,628	9	$ 22,911	14	$ 4,408
5	$ 34,203	10	$ 19,640	15	$ 0

The down payment may be anywhere from 0 percent to 50 percent, but the concept works the regardless of the down payment.

I purchased my first real estate when I was 18 years old and if I could buy real estate then, you can certainly buy real estate now. I have purchased real estate every year since then in every economic climate.

My first property was a duplex so I could live in half and rent the other half. I purchased it from a woman who had recently been widowed. She only wanted about $1,500 down and she wanted to carry the note. Since I was self-employed, that kind of financing worked very well for me.

In the first year, I was able to convert the duplex into a triplex. As I thought about how this would increase my cash flow, I discovered the next wealth secret.

WEALTH SECRET #2: BUY CASH FLOW PROPERTIES

Real estate that doesn't produce a cash flow is much more of a speculation than an investment. Cash flow properties are ones where the expected rental income is enough to pay the mortgage payment (principal and interest), taxes, insurance, a reserve for maintenance and vacancy, while still having at least a small positive cash flow.

Let's take a look at that same house in terms of cash flow. A 15-year mortgage for $45,000 of OPM at 6 percent interest will have a payment of $380 per month.

Income - Monthly Rent		$ 700
Mortgage Payment	$ 380	
Taxes	$ 45	
Insurance	$ 45	
Maintenance Allowance	$ 50	
Vacancy Allowance	$ 50	
Total Expenses		$ 570
Positive Cash Flow		$ 130

Regardless of the down payment, the critical part is having a positive cash flow after all expenses. If there is, then the house passes a primary test as a potential investment. Generally, the higher the down payment, the higher the cash flow.

THE MOST PREDICTABLE WAY TO GET RICH IS TO BUY AND HOLD CASH FLOW PROPERTIES.

This relates to the first wealth secret in that we wish to use OPM not only to purchase the property, but to make the monthly payments and cover all of the expenses. If you succumb to the temptation to buy a property that does not have a positive cash flow, then you risk losing the property if you ever lack the ability to make up the shortfall each month.

I held that first property for a few years, then I sold it and made a nice profit. I purchased a fourplex, lived in one unit, held it for a few years, and realized that it had also appreciated in value. That was when I discovered another wealth secret.

WEALTH SECRET #3: REAL ESTATE PRICES GO UP (APPRECIATION)

The value of real estate generally goes up, and it almost always goes up over a 15- to 20-year period of time. We call this "appreciation".

Let's take a look at how that same house appreciates over a 15-year period. We'll say that home values are steadily increasing by 5 percent per year, and see what the value of that house is at the end of each year.

Year	House Value	Year	House Value	Year	House Value
1	$ 52,500	6	$ 67,005	11	$ 85,517
2	$ 55,125	7	$ 70,355	12	$ 89,793
3	$ 57,881	8	$ 73,873	13	$ 94,282
4	$ 60,775	9	$ 77,566	14	$ 98,997
5	$ 63,814	10	$ 81,445	15	$ 103,946

Here's another way to look at it:

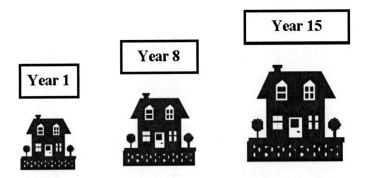

I began to realize that this real estate thing was even better than I had expected - and another wealth secret was right in front of me.

WEALTH SECRET #4: EQUITY MULTIPLIER EFFECT

If I combined the concepts of appreciation and OPM, I could literally double the rate at which my wealth would grow.

Year	Mortgage Balance	House Value
1	$ 43,091	$ 52,500
2	$ 41,064	$ 55,125
3	$ 38,913	$ 57,881
4	$ 36,628	$ 60,775
5	$ 34,203	$ 63,814
6	$ 31,628	$ 67,005
7	$ 28,895	$ 70,355
8	$ 25,992	$ 73,873
9	$ 22,911	$ 77,566
10	$ 19,640	$ 81,445
11	$ 16,167	$ 85,517
12	$ 12,479	$ 89,793
13	$ 8,565	$ 94,282
14	$ 4,408	$ 98,997
15	$ 0	$ 103,946

If I sell the property after fifteen years, that $103,946 is all my money, since the mortgage is now completely gone. That's $103,946 is in my brick and mortar savings account.

I was excited! I was living for free and still enjoying a small positive cash flow, but I realized that I was moving very slowly toward my goal of becoming a millionaire. I owned a nice fourplex, but since it was only worth about $80,000, I was only enjoying equity buildup (through debt reduction using OPM) and appreciation on that one $80,000 property.

Suddenly, the last of the five wealth secrets was obvious: I needed to repeat the process.

WEALTH SECRET #5: THE COOKIE CUTTER METHOD

That's right. All I had to do was repeat the process. Just like a cookie cutter makes identical copies of cookies, I needed identical copies of my rental house. If I had more real estate, I'd be enjoying debt reduction and appreciation on more real estate.

I have honed this to what I call the 10/5 formula. It's a simple concept. If you purchase just ten cash flow properties costing $50,000 each, within a five-year period, and hold those properties, you should be a millionaire in fifteen years or less.

Of course, you don't have to stop at ten properties, or buy them at just two properties per year. You can proceed as fast or as slow as you choose, and you can grow as big as you want.

Look at what happens when you multiply the first example by ten.

Year	Debt	Value
1	$ 43,091	$ 52,590
8	$ 25,992	$ 73,873
15	$ 0	$103,946

1 House

10 Houses

Year	Debt	Value
1	$ 430,910	$ 525,000
8	$259,920	$ 738,730
15	$ 0	$ 1, 039,460

CONGRATULATIONS!

YOU HAVE BECOME A REAL ESTATE MILLIONAIRE!

GETTING GOVERNMENT MONEY

I told you at the beginning that I collect about $2 million a year in rent from the government. That is because I own about 600 unites, most of which are single-family houses. I have been a landlord for over 35 years, but I only reached 100 properties about fifteen years ago. The big growth in the last fifteen years has been due to focus and systems. A lot of that focus and systems-building has been centered on being able to collect rent from the government using a program called Section 8.

The Section 8 program is a federally funded, locally administered housing assistance program for low-income people. These people choose where they would like to live, and they can ask any landlord to participate in the program. After the tenant and landlord have both agreed to work together, a three-way agreement is executed between the landlord, the tenant, and the local agency. After that, the government generally pays the majority of the agreed-upon rent directly to the landlord.

Now the great thing about this program is that you're dealing with the government. The checks are always on time, and they never bounce. There is no hassle in collecting the lion's share of the rent and the smaller remaining portion of the rent is usually easier to collect.

The challenging thing about this program is that you're dealing with the government. You have probably had some experience dealing with the government at some level. You have probably experienced at least a little frustration as you discovered that they are occasionally inflexible and seemingly irrational. The Section 8 program is no exception.

If you are like many people I have spoken to, your mind quickly came up with some objections to considering the Section 8 program. Here are the answers.

- Yes, you sti very highest-quality housing.)

WHAT I LIKE BEST ABOUT THE SECTION 8 PROGRAM

I discovered many years ago that the tenants who had been with me the longest tended to be the tenants that were on Section 8. As I analyzed my business, I realized that, as a landlord, my biggest enemy is turnover.

Many expenses, such as cleaning and repair, only occur when the tenant vacates a property. Vacancy, and the resulting lack of rental income, begins with turnover.

Obviously, the lower a tenant's income, the more difficult it is for them to pay the expenses associated with moving. Also, if they have a nice place to live and only have to pay 10 percent of the rent, they probably aren't very motivated to move. These are the reasons why Section 8 customers stay longer.

Other benefits to the landlord include ease of rent collection, predictability of rent collection, an increased number of potential customers, and a third party who

sometimes encourages the tenant to fulfill their obligations to the landlord.

Although I have worked with the Section 8 program for 30 years, the first 15 years were not happy. It was my fault. I kept trying to get those government administrators to do things my way. As you can imagine, what I mostly got was indigestion. When I chose to pursue these tenants more vigorously, I also chose to change my approach in dealing with the program.

The secret is to thoroughly understand their rules and regulations. You wouldn't try to play baseball without first learning the rules, and you wouldn't try to convince the umpire to change the rules to suit you. Since you're reading this book, you can apply this concept without the 15 years of heartburn it took me to begin using this secret.

DEVELOP GREAT SYSTEMS

Especially if you are working with the Section 8 program, and even if you aren't, you cannot overestimate the importance of having a plan and of having systems. There have been times when I have had to stop buying properties just because my systems were overloaded. That's a nice way of saying that I had lousy systems. From your very first rental, you will begin to appreciate the value of great systems or experience the pain of poor systems.

I have made more than two-thirds of my progress as a real estate investor in the last one-third of my investing career. This exponential growth began when I developed a focused plan. I am quite confident that you can double or triple your

ROBERT ELDER

progress if you have a focused plan and use systems to build
your real estate wealth.

It has been said that one of the best ways to learn
something is to teach it. I teach what I'm talking about here.
I also teach other techniques, such as how to keep buying
after you run out of cash, that can save you years of slow
growth and hundreds of thousands of dollars. As with any
mentor, if you do exactly what I do, you will get the exact
same results.

Approximately 12 years ago, I started a real estate investor
association called MILLIONAIRE POSSIBILITIES which
meets once per month. The purpose is to help create real
estate millionaires by sharing information and helping
people make the contacts they need. We are presently in
the process of making this information available online
at www.millionairepossibilities.com or www.mpmeeting.
com (they are the same site - one is easier to remember
and the other is easier to type). Soon there will be many
tools available online to help investors. We meet on the first
Thursday of every month. Millionaire Real Estate Club
(www.millionairerealestateclub.com) is the next step for
investors who are committed to being a real estate millionaire
or multimillionaire.

I offer a high-end coaching program for experienced
individuals who wish to jump-start their success or redirect
their investment business. This coaching and mentoring
program is highly individualized and creates rapid change
and exponential growth. For more information, you may call
my office at (405) 286-2000.

SUMMARY

- Holding cash flow rental properties is the most predictable way to get rich.
- There are five real estate wealth secrets:
  1. Use Other People's Money (OPM), first to initially fund each property and then to repay the loan.
  2. Only buy properties that have a positive cash flow.
  3. Appreciation happens without any effort from you.
  4. Combine OPM with appreciation to give you the ultimate wealth-building tool (Equity Multiplier Effect).
  5. Keep going until you have at least $500,000 in real estate and you will be a real estate millionaire before your toddler graduates from high school (Cookie Cutter Method).
- Consider letting the government pay you each month.
- Have a plan, be specific, and think BIG.

DEVELOP GREAT SYSTEMS AND CREATE FREEDOM, NOT JUST ANOTHER JOB.

JASON SIMPSON has been investing in real estate for over 10 years, and has successfully mastered a number of techniques including Wholesaling, "Subject To", Short Sales, Lease Options, Buy and Hold, and numerous other strategies. Jason has been a board member of his local Real Estate Investors Association for over 5 years.

After a challenging ordeal not related to real estate, Jason was forced to declare bankruptcy just over three years ago. After bankruptcy, Jason became an expert in dealing with lenders to purchase homes using none of his own cash or credit, quickly building his net worth into the hundreds of thousands. He is fast approaching millionaire status, all while working full time as a police officer. Jason helps others to learn how to invest in real estate, and has a burning desire to continue helping others that have faced similar situations. He has created a step-by-step formula to do this regardless of one's cash flow, credit history, or time schedule.

In his spare time, Jason enjoys spending time with his wife, Tracy, and their two boys, Preston & Logan. He also enjoys sailing in the British Virgin Islands, international travel, magic, and helping others achieve their goals and dreams through real estate investing.

Jason is currently offering his free "12-Part Mini E-Course on Real Estate Investing" to help people get started. The course can be found on his website at www.StreetCopMillionaire.com. Jason has also written an e-book on wholesaling properties, as well as a comprehensive course that covers Wholesaling, Obtaining the Money, and Buying & Holding!

If you have any questions for Jason, you can contact him at:

Street Cop Millionaire

P.O. Box 722194

Norman, OK 73070

Jason@StreetCopMillionaire.com

CHAPTER TWO

HOW A FULL-TIME COP IS MAKING A KILLING INVESTING IN REAL ESTATE PART-TIME

WHILE IT IS PRETTY EVIDENT that investing in real estate is a great way to go, I'm sure that a lot of you are wondering how to manage trying to build a successful real estate business while having a full-time career. Well, I've got a bit of experience in that, and hopefully in these next few pages, I can give you some ideas that will convince you that you can do this, too.

You might be in a different situation than I am. You may work more hours. You may have other things that you have to deal with. Whatever your situation is, you can work through it. That's the key. Now, let me just give you an idea where I'm coming from, and how I'm managing things.

First, I work full time as a police officer, and will at least until I'm vested, which will occur at my 10-year mark (October 2009). I work over 40 hours a week - well, 41.25 hours per week, not counting any overtime on calls that I might get. When I started investing in real estate, I worked part-time jobs on my days off. I worked at a bank, at a school, and at numerous other part-time "gigs". (You'll find that most police officers have part-time jobs to supplement their income.) My wife and I had made the decision that once we had kids, Tracy would stay home to raise them. We now have two wonderful boys and we stood by our decisions, although at first we were pretty financially strapped and had very little free time.

Since we began investing in real estate, I no longer have to work any extra jobs at the Police Department to make ends meet. Of course, real estate has taken the place of those extra jobs, but investing pays a lot better, which is why I began doing this. Investing in real estate is coming close to providing me with enough cash flow to decide if, when, and how much I want to work (it's pretty hard for me to consider my investing real work) and to spend time with my family.

Enough of my background. Let's move on. I'll tell you how I accomplished it, and I'll give you some tips on how you can do the same.

What I love about real estate is that you can fit your work into little bits of time - if you do it correctly! Now, if you decide to start off with a huge rehab job with no education or experience, it will end up biting you in the end. That's absolutely the last project I would advise you to start, both in terms of risk and time.

EDUCATE YOURSELF

First, you're definitely going to need to get some education. While I love investing and have tons of courses and training material, the biggest mistake I could make would be to think that I know all there is to know about investing. I suggest you make it a point to enjoy learning, because it will pay you massive dividends.

Now, most cops listen to the radio when they are driving around on patrol. Instead of that, I turned a disadvantage into a huge advantage and put all of my courses on my iPod and spent eight hours a day listening to information that would grow my mindset. Although I don't imagine that most of you have eight hours a day to listen to educational stuff - and I'll be honest, there were some days when the last thing I could listen to was something about real estate - I would recommend that, whenever you're driving around, you listen to something that will help to educate you or propel you toward your goals as opposed to music day in and day out. This is a huge key to success!

If you have limited time, you have to make it a point to make the most of the time that you do have. Even if you're only driving to work for 10 to 20 minutes a day, you also have 10 to 20 minute to drive back, so you have 20 to 40 minutes a day to educate yourself. If you have errands that you have to run, that could grow your listening time even more.

Let's add it up: 20 minutes x 5 days (a typical work week) = 100 minutes x 50 weeks = 5000 minutes, or over 83 hours per year! If your travel time is longer than that, you've just bumped it up even more! Little bits of time add up immensely! Think about moments when you are wasting your time and find a way to use them to bring you closer

to where you want to be. Do you have any books in the bathroom? Why not?

FIND THE TIME

Your next step is to leverage your time. I don't know your exact situation, so I'll just imagine that you're starting from scratch like I did, with little cash and very little time. You may be a step or two ahead, and if so, then you can adjust accordingly.

I would highly recommend that you make a time chart and account for every minute of every day for a week. Just make a diary of what you do during every half hour. Now, if you're an average person, you probably waste enough time watching TV, surfing the Internet, reading newspapers, or reading e-mail - time that could make you millions in real estate investing, if you could only apply it correctly.

EVERYTHING YOU DO IS EITHER MOVING YOU TOWARD YOUR GOAL OR AWAY FROM IT. PERIOD.

So, take a week and journal exactly where your time is going. You will be amazed at how much time you're wasting. I know I was! Once you do this, you'll have an idea of where your time is being wasted. It might not be much, but it's something. Your job is to find that time, and schedule it for developing your real estate investing business. It doesn't matter if it's reading a book, going to lunch with an investor, going to a local REIA meeting, making offers, or whatever.

You just have to start where you are, and plan time to do it. And then….JUST DO IT! Pick a set amount of time that you want to use for your freedom, and make it part of your schedule.

Once you have an idea of how much time you're wasting, you have to figure out how you can begin investing with your limited time. The quickest and easiest way that I have found to invest with the least risk, effort, and time is by wholesaling, or flipping houses.

Now, I'm not talking about the type of "Flip This House" kind of flipping that you see on TV where they do a complete rehab. That's the last thing I'd point you toward. I'm talking about finding a deal, locking that deal up, and passing it along to someone that's looking for a deal! That was what gave me the belief that I could do this thing, and on my first deal, I made $5,000 (about six weeks of my policeman's salary at the time) with about eight hours of work. I did it all wrong, and I spent way too much time on that one - no joke! But I did learn from my mistakes.

Instead of showing homes, now I stick a lockbox on the property, take calls, and give people the code. That's a huge time-saver for me. If you have very little time and can't answer calls because you have a job, then you have to adapt and overcome that limitation any way that you can!

Here are some other time-savers that I have implemented.

Instead of taking calls about each property personally, set up an outgoing voice mail message and use it as an advertisement. If they are interested in more info, have them leave a message to call you back. Now, that's not necessarily the best thing to do, but it is something, and what I have found

is that doing something is always better than doing nothing! If you make a continuous effort in the bits and pieces of time you have, and do it on a consistent basis, then you will eventually be rewarded.

Once you have done a couple of deals, you will want to reinvest that cash into making you more productive. That could be hiring someone to put up bandit signs for you, hiring someone to take the calls for you, implementing a website with a back-office management side to help you leverage your time, or whatever else boosts your productivity.

Your end goal, if you're anything like me, is to establish a business that will provide you with cash flow every single month, whether you are at home or on a beach somewhere, sipping mixed drinks. The key to getting to that point is implementing a system.

CASH FLOW

Personally, while I like to suggest wholesaling to help people get started, I am of the opinion that you're only as good as your next deal. It can bring some great cash, and it's a great way to get your feet wet when learning this business, but once the deals stop, the cash stops as well.

In my case, I'm focusing on getting my cash flow by buying and holding properties, renting them out while continuing to wholesale and do other deals on the side. This enables me to have a consistent cash flow every month. While cash will help to get you started, eventually you'll understand that it's not cash that's king, it is cash flow. Cash flow buys me time to do what I want, and that's spending time with my family.

Now, there are literally thousands of ways to make money by investing in real estate. When you get started, you'll identify the niche that you most enjoy, and that's where you want to focus your efforts. I do know successful investors that only wholesale, but they have a system in place with others doing a lot of the legwork so they don't have to do it.

When you are getting started, it is important to think of the big picture. Think about what systems you can implement to take "you" out of the picture which will also allow the cash flow to continue. Of course, if you're just starting, you'll want to keep "you" in the picture to further your education. If you take "you" out too soon, then you run the risk of not being able to determine when things are going smoothly, or when something is wrong. There is a value in knowing your business, but you will eventually want to move beyond this to eventually work on your business as opposed to working in your business.

THE BEST WAY TO START THE DAY

Another tip that I highly recommend is using the power of positive questions. Now, this isn't necessarily the positive thinking mumbo jumbo (although I do firmly believe that positive thinking is better than negative thinking), but rather realizing that *you will move toward what you focus on*. So, although you might have to get up early and go to work whether you enjoy your job or not, why not start off the day right?

I recommend asking yourself some "Power Questions" each day so that you can help your mind to focus on that which pulls you toward your goals as opposed to that which takes you away from them. Some examples could be:

- What am I going to do today to increase my knowledge about real estate investing?
- What property can I make an offer on today?
- What can I do today to find a new deal?

I think you get the point! "What am I going to…", "How can I…" , etc., are some great ways to begin your "Morning Power Questions".

At the end of the day, you can ask yourself some "Evening Power Questions" to reflect on the day's events. Some examples of these could include:

- What did I do today to increase my knowledge about real estate investing?
- What did I do today to propel me forward and assist me in finding another deal?
- What did I do today to increase my net worth and/or cash flow?

Those questions will help keep you accountable to your goals.

Now, while this isn't necessarily a "Goal Planning" session, it's important to realize that when you have goals, a strong desire to reach your goals, and a detailed vision of what exactly it is that you want, then you will be more motivated to do what it takes, especially if you have to find bits and pieces of time to accomplish it.

TIME MANAGEMENT

One of the biggest things that I used to help me manage my time was to implement the Franklin Covey system. Preferably at the end of the day, before you go to bed, write a

list of the things that you need to do the following day. These items or tasks can typically be divided into four categories: Urgent/Important, Urgent/Non-Important, Non-Urgent/Important, and Non-Urgent/Non-Important.

Examples of these could be the following:

- **Urgent/Important:** Make the car payment, finish a work report that's due tomorrow
- **Urgent/Non-Important:** Make a phone call interrupting your activity
- **Non-Urgent/Important:** Prepare your will, get your yearly physical, work out
- **Non-Urgent/Non-Important:** Watch TV, surf the Net

Typically the most important tasks are the Non-Urgent/Important tasks, with the Urgent/Important tasks pretty close in importance.

So, make that list of all the items that you want to complete the following day. The way I typically do it is that, after making this list, I categorize the items with a letter A, B, C, or D. A means that this is an item that you must get done. B is an item that you should get done. C is for items that you could get done, but aren't necessarily needed. Finally, D means that this item is trivial. Next, write numbers next to each item in each section, in the order that you want to complete them, giving the most important item the number 1. Then, when tomorrow comes, you start with A1 and work on it till it's completed, then you move to A2, and so forth.

I do recommend that you do this every evening so that your subconscious mind can work through it as you sleep, and you will be more prepared when the day begins.

This idea has been around for ages, and it is so simple that it's scary. I do highly recommend that you check out your local office supplies store for Franklin Covey products, and look into getting their planning system/calendar. It is a great investment and a great time-management system, and it has allowed me to be much more productive with bits and pieces of time than I would have been otherwise. The key is to get into the habit of using it.

It's also important to look at people who have had it worse than you do who have succeeded! No matter the situation, you can always find people in worse shape than you who have overcome their issues and have moved forward. Some people have tremendous health issues that they have overcome, others have had severe financial setbacks, and others have had to battle time-management issues. Look for people that have been worse off than you currently are, and use their successes to help motivate you to get the job done. "If he can do it, then I sure as heck should be able to as well!"

For me, I think the single thing that had the biggest impact was realizing that there was no task too small that didn't matter. I have firmly come to the conclusion that taking a series of little actions add up to big results. In my opinion, it's not an "Additive Effect", but more of a "Multiplying Effect" , where three actions plus three actions don't equal six actions, but end up coming out to nine. Something that may appear to be a small action internally may end up having a huge effect in the outside world.

It's like dropping a pebble in the water. While the pebble is small, that single pebble can have multiple ripples that can go for great distances. There's an old saying that a butterfly flapping his wings can cause a ripple so far away that it will

cause a tsunami thousands of miles away. You never know what your continuous small actions will lead to!

FIVE THINGS, EVERY DAY

If I were to wrap this up in a single bit of advice, it would be this: Don't end each day without doing five things to further your business. It doesn't matter if they are small or big. I don't mean "getting things organized so that you can get started", I mean actions that will provide you with results.

Depending on your experience, this could be reading part of a book on investing for ten minutes, listening for twenty minutes to a training program, making an offer on a property, preparing a mailout, looking at deals on the MLS, signing a lease with a new tenant, putting an ad in the paper, hanging bandit signs, closing on a deal, etc. The list of what you can do is huge - just don't get that mixed up with trivial junk that doesn't amount to much more than paper shuffling and busy work that doesn't get you anywhere.

Now, keep in mind that you can't just read, read, read, read, and read for your five things, unless you're brand spankin' new at this. Take an action to get ahead. Get some business cards out, order business cards, farm your target area - seriously, the tasks you could do are endless, and most of them take a very short amount of time to complete, or at least begin. You may even find that you only have to use a quarter of your wasted time each day!

What's the key? It's not the "five things". It's the *every day*". Sure, you can take your weekends off, but I don't recommend it. You spend 40 hours a week or more working

for someone else. Why not spend some time working for your freedom?

If you're anything like me, what you will find is the following: When you make it a constant habit to work towards something, bits and pieces of time will free up. In the general order of things, I think that it is a fundamental law that consistent action is rewarded. The amount of the action isn't important...the consistency of it is.

By consistently using the little bits and pieces of time that are typically wasted, that small amount of action will have a huge effect on the "big picture" and take you much further than if you used huge chunks of time, but were inconsistent in doing so. I would gladly take twenty minutes a day over a four-hour time slot every two weeks, and could accomplish more by focusing during that twenty minutes. It's amazing what you can do in a short amount of time when you focus on it.

I hope that you've gleaned something from this chapter that you can immediately apply in your own real estate investing endeavors. If you enjoyed the tips, I'd like to invite you to check out my free "12-part Mini E-course on Real Estate Investing" at www.StreetCopMillionaire.com!

Remember...just five things a day, *every day*. Even if you can't manage to do five, do something - anything. Do something every day to bring you closer to your goals. Small things lead to big, big results! Nobody is going to do it for you! What are YOU going to do today?

FRANK AUFIERO is a true real estate entrepreneur and mentor. He has been at the forefront of virtual real estate investing and currently has virtual assistants working for him in many capacities.

Frank started out with one vacant lot and turned it into a successful real estate career. He has successfully wholesaled over 200 vacant lots in Florida while living in Oklahoma City. He has rehabbed over thirty houses in the past three years and wholesaled over 100 homes in that time.

Frank went from nuclear medicine technology to full-time real estate investing and coaching. He is currently the owner of FLA LOTS, LLC, Talt Properties, LLC, www.smokinhotpropertyleads.com, and A. G. Home Solutions, LLC. His company, Talt Properties, LLC, is known in the Oklahoma City market as well as the Tampa Bay, Florida, market as a reliable source of wholesale real estate deals. He currently holds a few hundred thousand dollars' worth of real estate, owned free and clear, that pays him month after month.

Frank has successfully mentored students from many states. His most recent project, www.smokinhotpropertyleads.com, is a nationwide one-stop shop for buyers and sellers to meet in an online community setting and make deals happen. Frank is the real deal when it comes to real estate investing and coaching.

If you have any questions for Frank, you can contact him at:

(866) 919-8258 toll-free or

(405) 708-4768

www.lrnrealestate.com

www.smokinhotpropertyleads.com

www.taltproperties.com

www.flalotsllc.com

www.aghomesolutions.com

CHAPTER THREE

WHOLESALE YOUR WAY TO THE TOP!

THIS CHAPTER WILL TAKE YOU through the building blocks of your wholesaling business, detailing crucial steps of the business while also exploring your personal agenda. The greatest thing about the wholesale process is that you don't need to buy a house to make money on it!

WHOLESALING INVOLVES FINDING A BARGAIN PROPERTY AND PASSING THAT BARGAIN ON TO ANOTHER INVESTOR FOR A PROFIT.

Wholesaling should always be a part of your investment philosophy. You will literally be amazed at the opportunities you will find for wholesaling and the profits these deals can bring you.

Should you need fast cash, don't like the neighborhood, or don't have the dollars to fund the deal – wholesaling is the way to go.

Sometimes you buy a property and realize you may not have enough profit for you to rehab. Bail yourself out and wholesale. Sometimes you may just wholesale to provide a great deal to someone so they will come back!

FOUR BASIC STEPS TO A SUCCESSFUL WHOLESALE TRANSACTION

- Locate the right properties and the most motivated sellers.
- Determine the purchase price, market value, and final sales price.
- Attract buyers for properties once you have them under contract.
- Close your deal as quickly possible once you have assigned the contract.

"DO I HAVE TO USE MY OWN MONEY?"

The simple answer to that question is that you don't really need to have the money! So how can you still make a profit without really investing any money of your own? I have one short answer to that question: assignment of contract.

ASSIGNMENT IS WHEN YOU HAVE A CONTRACT TO PURCHASE A PROPERTY AND YOU ASSIGN ALL OF YOUR RIGHTS AND OBLIGATIONS OF THAT CONTRACT TO SOMEONE ELSE.

Why in the world would anyone assign their rights and obligations of a contract to a buyer? There is a little thing called an assignment fee and that, my future wholesaler, is your meal ticket. Every time you assign a contract, you may charge an assignment fee, which can be whatever the market bears.

Once you assign a contract to a buyer, they will be responsible for bringing the money to closing. You will be paid by the title company at the close. Your income will appear on the HUD-1 statement as an assignment fee.

TYPES OF PROPERTIES TO WHOLESALE

Most investor make the mistake of only wholesaling low-end, ugly houses. While you can wholesale $5,000 houses, you can also wholesale $500,000 houses. We like to stay in the range of $20,000 to $70,000 houses, however. We have made up to $75,000.00 in one wholesale transaction. Other types of properties that we have wholesaled include Commercial, Multifamily, and Vacant Land (my favorite).

WHO ARE MY BUYERS?

Broadly speaking, you have a few types of buyers:

- Investors who want to buy & re-sell, or what we call rehabbers
- Investors who are landlords and want to hold
- Owner-occupants who want to live in the house (more difficult - banks don't like assignments)

WHICH ARE THE BEST WHOLESALE DEALS?

I prefer "subject to" deals because the buyer gets in with very little down and sets up a land trust, takes over the seller's payments, and walks into a lot of equity. These houses sometimes bring over 100 percent return on investment (ROI), and sometimes more like 300 percent ROI or more.

When the buyer wants to get in light and you have a smoking hot wholesale deal, it is a win-win situation. You make your assignment fee, and they get a house at way below market value.

I like to stick with median-priced houses in good areas which require minimal repairs.

WHAT CAN I EXPECT TO PROFIT ON A DEAL?

Profit margins vary on every property. While some have fetched me $1,000, others have raked in as high as $75,000. On average, you could expect to profit between $5,000 and $10,000 per deal.

A formula I generally use to figure my assignment fees is 10% of the selling price.

HOW IT WORKS

You do not need to acquire the title to a property to wholesale it. Once you have a contract on a property with a seller, you will assign that contract, your rights, and your liability (if structured correctly) to the purchaser. The purchaser in turn will close directly with that seller. You will be sent an IRS Form 1099 from the title company on all wholesale deals, so you must keep track of all your deals.

CHECKLIST FOR WHOLESALING

Here's a quick walk-through of things you would need to do as you prepare yourself to wholesale:

- Locate seller.
- Determine ARV (after repaired value) for the property.
- Work on getting the property under contract. We always try for sixty days; however, if we can get longer, we will.
- Determine your sales price.
- Shoot out to buyers' list, make flyers, put out bandit signs, and run ads.
- Get purchase (assignment of contract).
- Send contract and assignment to title company of choice.
- Coordinate buyer and seller for closing.
- Go to closing and pick up your check.

```
┌─────────────────────────────────────────────┐
│                                               │
│        ASSIGNMENT INCOME                      │
│                                               │
│    Contract Amount:        $50,000            │
│                                               │
│    Buyer Pays:             $55,000            │
│                                               │
│    Your Assignment Fee:    $ 5,000            │
│                                               │
└─────────────────────────────────────────────┘
```

SETTING UP YOUR COMPANY

Processes and systems are essential for the smooth and efficient functioning of your business. Let's look at where you can begin:

- Secure your domain name at www.godaddy.com.
- Create your own website(s) for real estate investing at http://investorpro.com. Save $50 here with my coupon at http://investorpro.com/talt.
- Design your post cards at www.vistaprint.com.
- There are many places to buy bandit signs. We use www.signelect.com.
- To set up your company quickly, you can contact www.amerilawyer.com.
- We get inexpensive phone lines at www.voicenation.com.
- To set up free office lines or VOIP, contact www.skype.com.

- To blast our entire e-mail list, we use www. constantcontact.com
- Register your company with Dun & Bradstreet and begin building business credit at www.dnb. com.

BUILD DATABASE 101

A database of buyers and sellers is critical for your business. A few examples of the databases we build include absentee owners, *list pendants*, divorces, probates, and many more.

Below are a few website companies who can put databases together for you.

- www.dataquick.com
- www.listsource.com
- www.realquest.com

USING A PRE-SORT COMPANY

We use a pre-sort company. Bring them a database CD and they do all the work. You can also use www.click2mail. com. Use their post cards, upload your list, and click once to send them all. It's easy.

VIRTUAL ASSISTANTS

Get someone to help you out while you handle the more important tasks - hire a Virtual Assistant (VA). Thank goodness for the global economy! We have at least three virtual assistants working on different projects at any one time. Some of the responsibilities you can give your VA are

doing your due diligence, researching databases, and creating spreadsheets for your mailing lists. There are hundreds of tasks they can do for you.

In order to find VAs for real estate, just do a Google search. We have some virtual assistants hired at $2.22 per hour. These assistants can do anything from post your real estate ads to research - almost anything you can imagine.

LOCATE PROPERTIES

Driving for Dollars is a technique that we use in our business on a weekly basis. Get in your car, bring a note pad and pen, and drive around looking for vacant or abandoned houses. You can pick out these houses in a number of ways: high grass, boarded-up homes, stickers on the windows from the city or county. Keep track of those addresses on your note pad so, when you get back to the office, you can begin the search for the owner of the property. In most states, this can be done on the county property assessor's website. Look up the address of the property and determine the name and address of its owner. Mail the owner a postcard stating something like, "We Buy Vacant and Abandoned Houses," or "We Buy Unwanted Houses," or "Tired of Being a Landlord? Sell Us Your Home and Get Cash Fast!"

Target areas where your buyers are looking for properties. For example, if you have a buyer that likes rentals in the southwest part of town, then blanket that area for a wholesale deal. The best way to wholesale is with the end buyer in mind.

Direct mail campaigns involve mailing letters out to groups of people such as recent *list pendants* filings, divorces,

or probates, to name a few. These people generally have houses that they need to sell.

Sheriff's Sale Lists are another great way to grab a property quickly and wholesale to a motivated seller.

Dilapidated housing lists are an excellent source of properties that can be wholesaled.

There is one website that will get you awesome deals and is a must for any investor. We like www.smokinhotpropertyleads.com for nationwide wholesale deals. It is a free community for investors. You can create a profile, add friends, and network like crazy. Build your list of buyers and - most of all - list your wholesale deals *absolutely free.*

Advertise that your company buys houses. Bandit signs are a great means of doing this; however, be careful where you locate these signs as some states have strict laws prohibiting these signs.

DETERMINE THE PROPERTY'S VALUE

Get as much information as you can possibly collect from your motivated sellers - the more the better. Always ask, "What do you **need** to get for the property?" At this point, you will determine the value of the property and see if a deal can be made.

Again, the best way to get a quick assessment of the value of a property is to look it up on the county assessor's website. You can also go to www.cyberhomes.com, www.realquest.com, and www.mls.com. Nothing beats Realtor® comps. This means that you are looking for comparable sales, or the value of similar homes on the market in that area. You are

looking for homes which are active, pending, or have been sold in the past 90 days. Partner with a Realtor to help you with the MLS.

HOW DO YOU KNOW HOW MUCH TO OFFER FOR A HOUSE?

If the comps bring the house in at $100,000, a general formula for wholesaling is to multiply $100,000 by .65 (65 percent) to get $65,000. From this, subtract the cost of the repairs and the assignment fee to get the top offer you will make on that house.

THE TOP OFFER FORMULA	
$100,000 x .65	$65,000
Repairs	- $7,000
Assign fee	- $5,000
Best Offer	$53,000

You can always bring your contractor with you to the house and tell them what you want done. A very generic way of estimating cosmetic-only rehabs (paint, carpet, minor repairs, counter tops, sinks, faucets, vinyl) is to simply allow $10 per square foot. If air conditioning, electrical, plumbing, or roofing is needed, then your contractor can help you figure that into your estimation.

REPAIR ESTIMATION EXAMPLE

Let's look at an example. You found a house which has been appraised at 1,200 square feet. The house is in generally good condition - no major items will be needed to sell this house on retail market. Multiply 1200 by $10 per square foot, and you get $12,000 in estimated rehab costs.

Note: This is very generic and basic. You can sometimes get this done for as little as $6 per square foot with your regular contractors.

USING OPTIONS

One advantage of an option contract is that it gives you the right to control the property for a period of time without the obligation of purchasing the property. You want to offer the seller the smallest amount of consideration as possible ($100, for example). Each state has a legal minimum, so check with your state's laws. Option contracts are great for pre-foreclosures, properties which you are unsure if you can move, and other situations.

SO WE HAVE A CONTRACT - NOW WHAT?

Find a buyer!

Newspaper advertising is a great way to locate buyers for your wholesale deals. Some newspaper ads that we run include such wording as "Owner Desperate", "Must Sell", or "Any Offer Considered". These advertisements are not meant to sell a property, but to locate investors who are looking to buy. Once you get a call, add these investors to

your list of buyers immediately. Keep a database of buyers' e-mail addresses and notify them as you get properties.

Your marketing strategy can include www.listsource. com, door hangers, flyers, Realtors, mortgage brokers, and attorneys.

Compose an e-mail to your investor list, giving the estimated value of this property as well as the estimated repairs that will be needed. Add pictures if possible.

Call your top five investors and tell them you're going to give them first shot at the property.

Go to local Real Estate Investors Association (REIA) meetings.

Check the county property appraiser's website for landlords (owners of more than one property) in that particular neighborhood.

Send flyers to local Realtors that may just have investors waiting for these houses.

Search Craigslist (www.craigslist.org).

BRING IN THE MONEY

In closing, there are so many opportunities to make money wholesaling real estate. We wholesale over 70 percent of our properties. This can be a useful technique to add to your real estate arsenal. You can't buy every house that comes your way, but that doesn't mean you cannot make money wholesaling it to the next investor looking for a rental in the area of your property.

BENEFITS OF HAVING A MENTOR

Have you ever thought about getting help from a mentor? When leads come in, let me help you evaluate them. E-mail me your deals and questions, or you can call me up to two times a week between 8:30 a.m. and 3:30 p.m. Central Time. All e-mails and calls will be answered within 24 hours!

RODNEY MILLER *is an author, speaker, and mentor to other real estate professionals. He is the CEO of Mig Properties LLC, a real estate investment firm located in Oklahoma City, OK.*

Rodney began his real estate career in 2002 with Homevestors Inc., a national home-buying franchise based out of Dallas, Texas. He branched off on his own in 2004 and has completed over 200 profitable real estate transactions since that time, establishing himself as a dominant force in the Oklahoma market.

Rodney often speaks to and mentors other real estate investors on a wide variety of topics, including raising private money, buying "subject to", buying and selling with owner financing, controlling properties with options, holding rental properties, wholesaling, flipping, quick-turn real estate procedures, real estate office procedures, systems, and employee management.

If you have any questions for Rodney, you can contact him at:

Mig Properties LLC

820 NW 13th Street

Oklahoma City, OK 73106

(405) 228-4906

CHAPTER FOUR

HOW I RAISED OVER TWO MILLION DOLLARS IN PRIVATE MONEY

In over seven years of real estate investing and coaching, the number one problem that I encounter from my students and fellow investors is in the area of financing their transactions. Let's face it - the best deal in the world isn't a deal unless you can come up with the money to fund the transaction. If you are going to buy houses at 50 cents on the dollar, you must have access to capital. Private lenders are the best source for that capital. Let me start by giving my definition of private lending:

PRIVATE LENDING IS A LOAN TRANSACTION BETWEEN TWO PARTIES WHICH DOES NOT INVOLVE A FINANCIAL INSTITUTION (BANK OR MORTGAGE COMPANY).

Your typical private investor is someone with an IRA, a 401(k), or a substantial amount of money in cash, CDs, or money market accounts. A private lender can be anyone who wants a good return on their investment. The lender can be a relative, a friend, a college buddy, an acquaintance, or anyone who is introduced to you by one of them. Your job is to identify people who fit this description, seek them out, and teach them why they should invest their money in your real estate deals.

I have put your private money raising campaign into five steps. Each step is equally important and is an integral part of the process of raising private capital for real estate investing. These steps are:

- Educate Yourself
- Build Credibility
- Develop Your Loan Product
- Develop Your Lender Presentation
- Develop Outstanding Customer Service Skills

Take the time to use each of these steps, and watch your success grow!

STEP 1: EDUCATE YOURSELF

The key to raising private money is to establish yourself as an expert, not only in the field of real estate, but also in the area of investing money wisely. There is no way you can do this without studying. You have to be able to answer the questions that your lenders will no doubt ask you, and you will have to be able to answer them intelligently and without hesitation.

These are the areas of education that I believe you need to be familiar with in order to be an educated, informed borrower of private money:

Notes and mortgages

It is imperative that you understand real estate paperwork, such as notes and mortgages or trust deeds. These are the nuts and bolts of every financed real estate transaction. You need to know about amortization schedules, balloon notes, and the effects of simple interest versus compound interest.

Title Work

Title work is an integral part of any real estate transaction, especially when there is a lender involved. If you have been in real estate for any length of time, you already realize this fact and you are probably familiar with the title process. If you are not yet familiar with the title process, I recommend that you pay a visit to your local title company to learn the basics about how your transactions will work.

How will your lender fund the deal? Will they fund via wire transfer or cashier's check? Who will draft the note and the mortgage? How long will it take for your lender to get the title insurance policy after closing? These are questions that your private lender will eventually ask you, and you need to have the answers.

Investing a retirement account in Real Estate

This is a very important area in which you really want to spend some time researching - and when I say researching, I'm not talking about weeks, I'm talking a handful of hours. Most of your private lenders are going to be loaning money

out of their IRA or 401(k) retirement accounts. It is your job to not only tell them how to move their money into a self-directed IRA account, but also to warn them about the prohibited transactions. Once again, you need to position yourself as the expert. Don't worry, it's not that technical and it's easy to learn. In a matter of one or two hours, you will be an expert at the subject of using self-directed IRA money for real estate transactions. Most people don't even think it's legal to loan money out of an IRA account. You have to educate them!

Reference Material

To begin educating yourself, Google these terms:

- IRA
- Investing in Real Estate
- Private Mortgage Lending
- Making Private Mortgage Loans
- Self-directed IRA Custodian+Real Estate
- www.trustetc.com (click the Education Center link)

Study these great books and course materials:

- Jimmy Napier, *Invest in Debt*
- Dyches Boddiford, *The Investor's Guide to Discount Notes and Mortgages*
- Teri B. Clark and Matthew Stewart Tabacchi, *Private Mortgage Investing*

Read everything thoroughly, and make sure you understand it before you begin to educate others.

STEP 2: BUILD CREDIBILITY

The number one question that arises in someone's mind before they hand you a check is, "Is this guy for real? Is he credible or full of it?" You have to give them overwhelming evidence that you are a safe bet and that you are credible. Your private lender needs to know that you will keep your word.

Here's how prove to your private lender that you are credible and that people can rely on you to handle their investment dollars with prudence.

Develop References

You need as many character, business, and personal references as you can get. Great sources include your banker(s), your vendors, other investors - the more influence and stature your references have, the better your credibility will appear. In other words, don't use your yard man as a reference.

Develop Testimonials

Get as many testimonials as you can from as many people as you can. Once again, the more professional and the higher the stature of those people, the better you will look.

For example, when I first started out, one of my testimonials was this:

> *"I have made several loans to Rodney Miller over the years and have found him to be honest, ethical, and reliable."*
> - Jesse Cowan, Vice President, Stillwater National Bank

If you were on the fence, wouldn't that help you get off on the right side?

Highlight Your Past Performance

This is a great way to build your credibility. If you have completed some profitable real estate transactions, you need to highlight those in a presentation format. Show what you paid for the property, disclose your rehab costs (if any), outline your exit strategy, and reveal your profitable conclusion. If there was a lender or bank involved that was paid off, you definitely need to highlight that as well. This simply shows a potential lender that you know what you are doing.

Hard Money

If you don't have any deals under your belt, you might need to do some with hard money. I know - it's expensive and it should be your last resort, but it's a great way to get some deals under your belt. You can then showcase those deals to your private lenders, and use the hard money lender as a reference and/or a testimonial.

STEP 3: DEVELOP YOUR LOAN PRODUCT(S)

Okay - you have studied and you have built your credibility kit. Now you need to decide what you are going to ask for. In other words, what are your products? The best way for me to explain this is to highlight my most popular products.

10% simple interest-only payments with a five-year Balloon Loan

This means that, if someone loans me $50,000, they will make $416 per month in interest payments until the five-year balloon payment comes due or I sell the property (whichever comes first). At that time, they get their initial investment of $50,000 back; hence, the term 'interest-only'.

12% Mezzanine Loan

I put this loan together to increase my cash flow. Although I am paying 12 percent interest, I only pay 6 percent monthly interest on the loan balance. The other 6 percent is accrued on the back end of the loan. This is great for holding rentals, as it allows for great cash flow.

STEP 4: DEVELOP YOUR LENDER PRESENTATION

You have now educated yourself, you have your references and testimonials, and you know what loan products you want to offer. Now it is time to work on your presentation. You have to boil down all of this information into a clear, concise sales pitch to your potential private lenders.

Elevator Speech

You will start with your elevator speech. An elevator speech is simply a 30- to 60-second sales pitch that you could squeeze into a typical elevator ride! It gives your prospect a good idea of what you are doing, how they can get involved, and what the benefits are to them. Use this speech casually at dinner parties, at your child's soccer game, to your CPA,

to your insurance agent, to your banker - you get the idea. Here is a sample:

"I'm a local real estate investor. I buy houses at fifty cents on the dollar and I borrow the money from private lenders. I pay 12 percent interest and secure each investment with a first mortgage on the property. You can use your IRA or 401(k) to invest with my company. I can show you how. If you're not making 12 percent on your money right now, we should talk further. I would be happy to buy you lunch and explain my program in more detail."

Now, obviously, you don't blurt this out. You wait for the right time to work it into the conversation. When people talk, they almost always get around to asking, "So what do you do for a living?" Time to pounce!

The Sit-down Meeting

I prefer lunch for a one-on-one meeting. It gives you a captured audience for about an hour, with an opportunity for some small talk to get to know your prospect. You will need either a laptop computer with a slide presentation or some handouts. Be sure that you have your testimonials, references, and past performance project overviews with you.

The Group Presentation

Once you have your one-on-one presentation down, a very simple next step is to prepare a group presentation such as a seminar or webinar. You can usually use the same PowerPoint presentation that you used for your sit-down meeting. Simply make your presentation to a group and let them ask questions afterwards. I suggest that you rent a conference room at a local golf course or country club and

have lunch provided for your attendees. You might even want to promote a free give-away drawing for all attendees just to get more interested parties to view the presentation. You might also want to consider having your CPA and/or your attorney with you to help build your credibility and to field any questions that may arise.

STEP 5: DEVELOP OUTSTANDING CUSTOMER SERVICE SKILLS

Finally, once you land a private lender, treat them like gold and do what you say you are going to do. Make their experience a positive one. Believe me, if you are giving them a 12 percent return on their money and you are on time with their payments every month, they will tell their friends about you.

You can increase your level of customer service a step further to ensure that they become raving fans. Your goal should be to go above and beyond your private lender's expectations. Wow them with customer service and let them know that you appreciate their business. Here are a few ways that you can show that your company is a well-oiled machine and not a 'Mom & Pop' operation:

Thank-you Letters

Always send a thank-you letter after a loan transaction is completed. You may even want to include a $50 gift certificate to a local restaurant to show your appreciation. Don't be cheap! These guys are your golden goose!

Follow-up Calls

Make a quarterly call to your lenders and invite them to lunch. If they are not in your area, just make the call to let them know that you are checking in. Ask them if they are happy with their investment, and find out if there are any improvements you can make in your system to service their account. If they give you some good ideas, you need to take action and implement them at once, if possible.

Keep Them Informed

If they loaned you money for a rehab, you should keep them updated with pictures of milestones on the project. Lenders love to watch their money at work. It makes them feel more involved in the deal. It also gives them something to show their colleagues, friends, and family, which leads to more potential lenders!

Cards

Always send Christmas and birthday cards to your lenders.

Stay in Touch

The best advice I can give you is stay in touch with your lenders as much as possible. This alone will give them more confidence in you and it will keep you on their minds, leading to more potential referrals.

Service Your Loans Like a Professional

Loan servicing is usually an afterthought to most real estate investors that want to raise private money. They land

their first private money transaction, the deal is funded, the house is purchased, and now the loan needs to be serviced. This is where they come to the realization that the loan isn't going to service itself.

What is loan servicing? Loan servicing is determining the details of the loan: the amortization schedule, the date the payments are due, where the payments are to be mailed, how much the late fees are, how the payments are tracked, and how the payoff amount is determined once the loan comes due.

There will be times when the lender calls and wants to know how much the payoff balance is, if the monthly payment went out on time, or when the balloon payment comes due. How do you keep up with all of this technical information? Use loan-servicing software.

Here are two accounting software programs that we use to keep track of our loan servicing. I highly recommend that you use *both* of them. They are affordable and very user-friendly.

Notesmith is an awesome accounting program for servicing loans. It is very simple to use. Set up the loan terms first. Every time you make a payment, you enter it into the system and it calculates the new balance for you automatically. It even does your year-end tax statements on interest paid.

T-Value is for setting up your loan scenarios. You can run several different loan scenarios, changing different factors such as interest rate, payment amount and balloon payments to create various amortization schedules. This is not for servicing loans, but it can help you view and analyze

different loan possibilities. It's a great tool to use, and it's fun to play with!

TAKE ACTION AND MOVE FORWARD

You now have the exact blueprint that I used to raise over two million dollars in private money.

Yes, it takes a little work, but I can tell you firsthand that it is 100 percent worth the effort. Once you develop a steady source of private lenders, you will be head and shoulders above the competition. You won't have to worry about where your next loan is coming from, you won't have to grovel to bank executives, and you won't have to wait for loan approvals from large committees.

There is a saying in the business world: "Cash is King". This is particularly true in the world of real estate investing. It is the investor with access to quick cash who lands the great deals. Now, get out there and line up your private investors!

CORY BOATRIGHT has been blessed to become an accomplished national speaker, real estate trainer and coach, professional writer, radio host, private consultant, and even a musician. He serves on the Board of Directors for a landlord and property investor association called "Millionaire Possibilities" (MPREIA).

Cory has been published in the Wall Street Journal for his successful business aptitude and continues to pursue real estate as a full-time investor and Loss Mitigation Specialist. He owns several companies, including a nationwide loss mitigation service with a team of full-time debt negotiators and a short sale marketing brand (ShortSaleology.com) that offers high-end coaching programs, software, and training programs. From synergetic team work, his exceptional team has successfully discounted millions of dollars in debt from hundreds of banks all over the country via short sales. He has personally bought and sold single family, multifamily, commercial property, and land.

Cory and his wife continue to buy and hold properties for long-term wealth planning, and to network with investors all over the world. At the age of 32, the biggest lesson he has learned in life is:

"Be a solutions provider by asking how you can serve one another better. The rewards of servant-hood are invaluable"

- Cory Boatright

If you have any questions for Cory, you can contact him at:

ShortSaleology.com

ATTN: Cory Boatright

Po Box 30906

Edmond, OK 73003

O: (888) 476-4114

F: (866) 211-0893

info@shortsaleology.com

CHAPTER FIVE

HOW TO GET A LENDER TO SAY "YES" TO A REAL ESTATE SHORT SALE

Nine Steps You MUST FOLLOW or Risk Failing

A "short sale" has certainly been a buzzword with all the foreclosures taking place in the real estate marketplace. Distressed homeowners are looking for creative ways to sell their homes quickly. However, many Realtors® and real estate investors are still unclear on how to get a lender to accept a real estate short sale offer.

The following nine steps are to be used as a guideline for determining what to offer the lender to get a short sale acceptance. This is not to be used as legal advice. It is recommended you have an educated real estate attorney on your investment team.

A SHORT SALE HAPPENS WHEN A LENDER AGREES TO THE SALE OF A HOME FOR LESS THAN IS OWED ON THE MORTGAGE.

Why would a lender take a loss on the mortgage? Approving a short sale costs them less money than they would have to spend to foreclose on the home.

To begin, here is a list of the things you will need to complete a short sale:

- Purchase and Sale Contract or Option to Purchase
- Notice of Option (filed at courthouse)
- Affidavit or Disclosure (cover your asset document)
- Authorization to Release
- Seller's Last Two Years' Tax Forms and W-2s
- Seller's Last Two Months' Bank Statements
- Seller's Last Two Months' Paystubs
- Financial Statement (use a standard FDMC form)
- Seller's Hardship Letter
- HUD-1 Settlement Statement (shows what the lender will net)
- Optional: MLS Listing Agreement and Buyer Preapproval Letter

STEP 1: DETERMINE FAIR MARKET VALUE (FMV)

The FMV can be determined by evaluating sold, comparable properties in a similar or close proximity to the subject short sale property. A Realtor will have access to the MLS (Multiple Listing Service) and can create a CMA (Comparative Market Analysis) for the subject property. This analysis will identify sold comparable properties with same square footage, bedrooms, baths, garage and other similar characteristics as your subject property. Request that the Realtor use a sold time frame of within the past six to twelve months when pulling properties in the immediate or surrounding areas. Usually, the short sale lender will not consider any sold comparable that are older than twelve months and that are further away than two miles from the location of the subject property.

STEP 2: EVALUATE SOLD COMPS SYSTEMATICALLY

Contrary to popular and often misguided belief, you can use a formulaic system to work in your favor when determining what to offer on the short sale property. This system has been around for years, but for some reason you may have not heard it mentioned in dealing with real estate. You will use the law of averaging. Here's how it works.

Let's say that you have eight sold comparable that are all similar in size, square footage, bedrooms, etc. This is how you apply the formula: take out the two highest comps and the two lowest ones, and average the rest.

ROBERT ELDER

Example

You determine that a property is worth $145,000. You have a Realtor pull a CMA and you find eight sold comparable properties that match the criteria above. The MLS (Multi Listing Service) shows the following:

$159,000	$148,000
$154,000	$143,000
$153,000	$146,000
$161,000	$151,500

Using our formulaic approach, you would take out the two highest sold comparable ($159,000 and $161,000). Then take out the two lowest sold comparable ($143,000 and $146,000). This would leave four others:

$154,000	$148,000
$153,000	$151,500

You would then take an average by simply adding up the sum of all the sold comparable and dividing them by the total number of properties left - in this case, that number would be four. $606,500 divided by four equals $151,625. Using this averaging formula, you can reasonably assume the house would sell for around $151,625 instead of the $145,000 you had originally estimated.

STEP 3: REVEAL THE ARV (AFTER REPAIR VALUE)

ARV is a slang term often used by real estate investors. It is similar to the FMV, but with a few differences. The ARV is calculated by the amount of repairs that the investor thinks the property needs in order to sell quickly on the open market using FSBO (for sale by owner) techniques and not using the MLS. It can be argued the ARV is more of a guess or suggested value derived by using sold comparable from houses that were not sold by a Realtor.

One way to explain the difference is that a Realtor will typically use a FMV (fair market value) evaluation method, while a real estate investor may elect to use an ARV. An appraiser can use both valuation methods, but generally sticks to the ones that come from the MLS. In my opinion, the ARV is a less accurate and less dependable value than those which come off the MLS. However, it is good to know both.

STEP 4: FIGURE OUT THE LENDER'S BPO

The BPO (Broker Price Opinion) is the single greatest value factor that the lender will use to determine the acceptance of your short sale offer. A BPO is a generalized opinion of the value of a property that the lender uses to determine what the property is worth. It is ordered by the lender and then sent to a third-party company such as BPO Direct, First America, Land Safe, etc. These companies have a list of Realtors in each state who work for them.

BPOs are ordered and conducted by Realtors. The BPO can be an Interior Type or Exterior Type. If an Exterior Type BPO is conducted, it means the Realtor (also known

as the BPO agent) did *not* go inside the property to evaluate its condition. This could be due to the homeowner vacating the house or not being cooperative with the BPO agent when a time was requested to inspect the house. Let's look at the different types of properties and how they are affected by the BPO.

STEP 5: WHAT IS THE HOUSE TYPE AND HOW DOES IT AFFECT THE BPO?

Dealing with "Pretty House" type short sales (categories will be defined later), you will find that the BPO will typically come in 10 to 20 percent lower than FMV or ARV. Based on this, you might consider offering 60 percent of the ARV or FMV value for your initial purchase offer.

Of course, this depends on the amount of repairs needed for the property. If you have what can be classified as a "Pretty House" type of short sale, which would show very little needed repairs, *do not* expect to get a huge discount from the lender for it. If you cannot justify a reason for the lender to accept a large discount (no supported sold comps anywhere near your offer price, no repairs needed, house has equity, house is in a great neighborhood and houses are selling fast there, etc.), don't expect the lender to give you one.

This also dispels the myth that all houses heading toward foreclosure are good short sale candidates. They are not.

Here is a good list of acceptable and non-acceptable short sale candidates.

Acceptable

- A hardship is preventing any more payments from being made to the lender.
- The homeowner is completely willing to work with you with no friction.
- The homeowner is already behind on mortgage payments.
- A *list pendant* has been filed at the courthouse.
- The bank has initiated the foreclosure process.
- The homeowner has no equity and the property is overleveraged, or the debt is more than it is worth.
- The property needs repairs.
- More than one mortgage is owed.
- One or more judgments or liens are owed.
- Property is listed for sheriff's sale with more than 10 days left to auction.

Non-Acceptable

- The homeowner is not compliant to requests for documents, showing their property, signing a listing agreement, etc.
- The homeowner does not have a legitimate hardship, but is using some excuse to not pay the lender when they have the money available.
- The property has a lot of equity, and the lender would be better off foreclosing to get paid in full.
- The sheriff's sale is less than 10 days away (avoid this if you don't want to stress yourself out).
- The homeowner requests to stay in the property.

Which deals should you pursue?

It is important that you do not waste your time with unwilling or unmotivated homeowners/sellers. They must be ready to leave the house for you to assist them with a short sale strategy. You cannot help all homeowners in or approaching foreclosure. You can only help those that are in complete compliance to your requests. You did not cause the homeowner to be in a hardship. If the short sale is not accepted, the homeowner's situation does not change.

The homeowner must have a legitimate hardship. The lender will not agree to a short sale if they believe the homeowner is just avoiding making the payments because they don't like the house anymore, they are upset at a spouse, they want to move quickly, or some other cop-out-type of excuse.

Don't waste time trying to assist homeowners that are not good short sale candidates. You are robbing the other people that are in desperate need of your help. Willing homeowners with legitimate hardships need a solution. Be a wise servant.

So, there you have it. If you are talking to a homeowner who makes plenty of money to pay bills, is a pain to work with, will not respond to your requests for paperwork, or wishes to stay in their house, move on. You are talking to an unacceptable short sale candidate. The better prospects are homeowners who have legitimate hardships, who have missed three or more payments, who are approaching foreclosure, whose property needs some repairs, and whose sheriff's sale is more than 10 days away from the auction date.

Cory's Short Sale Classifications

Here are some classifications and examples to make it easier to determine how much of a loss the lender may agree to accept.

- **PRETTY HOUSE**
- **UGLY HOUSE**
- **SCARY HOUSE**

A Pretty House is generally in a safe, desirable area where houses sell fairly quickly. If you find a house and its ARV/FMV is $100,000, for example, and you estimate that the repairs will cost between $5,000 and $10,000 (5 to 10 percent of the ARV/FMV), then your BPO will be between $80,000 and $90,000 (+/- 5 percent).

An Ugly House is generally a light rehab, a fixer-upper, or a handyman-special house in a fair neighborhood. You could find a house with an ARV/FMV of $100,000 (with Ugly Houses, this number tends to be the "as is" value instead of the ARV). You could estimate that the repairs will cost between $11,000 and $20,000 (11 to 20 percent), so your BPO will be $80,000 (+/- 5 percent).

A Scary House is generally a house that needs massive repairs and is located in an area that is not desirable, where lots of crime isn't uncommon. This house might have an ARV/FMV of $100,000 (with Scary Houses, this value tends to be the "as is" value instead of ARV), but the repairs should cost at least $35,000 (21 to 35 percent or more), which leaves you with a BPO of $65,000 (+/- 5 to 10 percent).

You can find a Scary House located in a great, fast-selling neighborhood and a combination of the others, but generally speaking, Scary and Ugly Houses will not be located in

excellent neighborhoods. Remember, this is a guideline, not an exact science. The BPO agent will generally consider the "as is" value for both Ugly and Scary Houses.

Now let's discuss the different loan types that the lenders will consider a factor per short sale submission.

STEP 6: LEARN THE LOAN TYPES

Here is the "skinny" on the different types of loans and how they will affect your short sale. When you learn these, you can increase your closing rate for a lender accepting your short sale by as much as 50 percent! Here's why: If you know more about any property, it provides you better leveraging and ultimately better negotiation strategies to target. Not all short sales are created equal.

Conventional loans

These loans are found all over the place. They provide the most flexibility, especially in dealing with short sales. Using the $100,000 Pretty House as an example, you might start out your offer by submitting 60 percent of the $100,000 FMV, which equals $60,000. The $60,000 is actually around 70 percent of the BPO price. However, it is very common to see the lender accepting around 80 to 85 percent of the BPO price, which in this case would be around $68,000 - $72,250.

This model can fluctuate a little bit, but this is a common average. The BPO (also considered the perceived value of the property), to the lender, is the main value factor. Therefore, in this example, if you thought the BPO was going to come in around $65,000, you would take 82 percent of that number, which would be $53,300. The lender may very

well accept $53,300 based on their perception of the value of the property.

This is not a scientific grading scale. It is the model used by many short sale investors as a guideline. You can and will have other factors that make you stray from this.

FHA loan

If you are dealing with an FHA loan, a VA loan, or any other government-backed loan, they are going to recoup a set amount of money if the foreclosure is completed. For example, with FHA loans, the insurer will basically guarantee the lender 82 percent of an FHA Certified Appraisal amount.

Notice that I did not write 'BPO amount'. For these loans, you will need an FHA Certified Appraisal for the lender to consider in the process of their evaluation of the property. The BPO will not suffice on these types of loans. You can massage the numbers from 1 to 2 percent, but 82 percent is listed in their guidelines.

- All FHA loans are insured by the federal government.
- As long as the lender follows FHA guidelines, they are guaranteed to net the percentages in their guidelines for the "as is" or appraised value.
- FHA-type loans will not use a BPO. Instead, they will require an FHA Certified Appraisal. Use the same techniques on the FHA Appraisal that you would for a typical short sale deal.

STEP 7: MEMORIZE THE PERCENTAGES

You must know the minimum accepted net offers of the BPO or FHA appraisal that the lender will consider. Here are the percentages you need to memorize:

Type of Loan	Percentage of BPO or FHA Appraised Amount
VA	82%
FHA	Net 88% - first 30 days of listing Net 86% - days 31 through 60 Net 84% - days 61 through 90
Freddie Mac (FDMC)	88% to 92%
Fannie Mae (FNMA)	85% to 88%
Conventional	80% (no set limit)

IMPORTANT: Understand that these are NET percentages to the bank. If you have your offers padded with things like Realtor commissions, closing costs and additional fees, these need to be included for the final net settlement.

Example #1

If an appraisal comes in for a VA loan at $200,000, the lender would consider accepting $164,000 (82 percent of $200,000) for it. Keep in mind, the $200,000 may or may not be the actual value of the property, but it will be the value the lender uses to determine how much they can discount.

Example #2

The BPO on one of your deals comes in at $100,000. Offers that may be accepted based on the above criteria would be:

Type of Loan	Percentage of BPO or FHA Appraised Amount	Acceptable Offer
VA	82%	$82,000
FHA (first 30 days of listing)	88%	$88,000
FHA (days 30 through 60)	86%	$86,000
FHA (days 61 through 90)	84%	$84,000
Freddie Mac (FDMC)	88% to 92%	$88,000 to $92,000
Fannie Mae (FNMA)	85% to 88%	$85,000 to $88,000

Some local banks, usually the smaller ones, will almost always refuse to allow more than a 10 to 15 percent discount off the property value, depending on the amount of repairs needed to fix it. Local banks tend to be more conservative in their approach to discounting the property. This is partly due to the network of local affiliates the bank can call to get more than one opinion of the repairs needed or the value of the property.

OK - now you know more than 90 percent of real estate investors. Let's keep moving and get you the acceptance letter.

STEP 8: HOW TO DEAL WITH JUNIOR LIENHOLDERS

If you are dealing with a junior lienholder such as a second mortgage, you are basically going to negotiate with them the same way as the primary/first lienholder. You will find that many junior lienholders will not require as much information to make a decision quickly on discounting their loan amount. They will generally order a BPO or have an appraisal on file. It could be an older or current one. Make sure and ask about it.

Sometimes a lender will actually tell you a BPO price. Now, before you get all excited and think, "This is GREAT!" - think again. Typically, loss mitigators will lie to you about the price and actually inflate it. Yeah, I know. You never thought lenders lied, did you? Well, they do, and they do it a lot.

When you are dealing with a first mortgage holder, it is not uncommon to find out that they will only allow $500 to $2,500 towards paying off any junior lienholders, judgments, etc. All lenders are a little different, but normally $1,000 is where they start. This is another reason why you will deal with more junior position lenders that are willing to take pennies on the dollar to satisfy their loan positions with the homeowner. In fact, you can often negotiate for 80 to 90 percent discounts or get approval for 10 to 20 cents on the dollar!

It can be beneficial if you get the primary lienholder to accept a short sale and then present that information to the

junior lienholder **IN WRITING!** If the primary lienholder is willing to take a deep discount, where does that leave the junior lienholder? As you can imagine, showing the junior lienholder that the primary lienholder has agreed to a short sale can be a powerful negotiation technique.

Remember, any junior lien holder who is holding an over-leveraged asset (the house) is in a *horrible* position. They realize this, and if you can build a strong case as to why it would be in their best interest to discount their position rather than risk losing *everything* at the foreclosure auction sale, it will generally not only help them, but it can make you, the investor, a huge pile of money, too.

Why? You just created equity out of thin air. That is the power of short sale negotiations.

STEP 9: YOU ARE EDUCATED

I just revealed to you what is probably the most concise definition of putting together an adequate short sale offer ever printed. The power of these steps, once put into action, can make their user extremely wealthy. Other real estate home study courses, books, and audios leave out what I just disclosed. This is the "meat" of preparing a satisfactory short sale offer.

There are no more secrets you need to know about doing short sales. I just shared them all with you. If you take the steps for preparing a short sale offer exactly as shown above and apply them in your real estate short sale business, the sky is the limit for your success in getting them approved.

"Cory Boatright is a flat out genius, yet he doesn't showboat all his wisdom like other gurus. His short sale

knowledge is unsurpassed and his team handles all our short sale work. Listen to him and take notes."

- Tim Mai, CEO of DoDeals.com and co-author of New York Times best-seller "The One Minute Millionaire"

Allen Moore is an author, coach and mentor to other real estate investors. He is the CEO of Buy It Kwik, LLC, a real estate investment company in Oklahoma.

In 2003, Allen lost his job. He had to support his family and did not have time to go back to college, nor could he afford a dead-end job with little pay. He looked into real estate and quickly found his calling. From having no prior experience in real estate, Allen has since completed over 150 real estate transactions to include wholesaling, "subject to", retail flipping, and buy-and-hold rentals.

Allen has partnered with other investors on many lucrative real estate deals and is always looking for more people who want to invest in real estate with him. Allen currently resides in Edmond, Oklahoma, with his wife, Vicki, and daughter, Megan.

If you have any questions for Allen, you can contact him at:

Buy It Kwik, LLC

P.O. BOX 1479

EDMOND, OK 73083

(405) 812-2274

Allen@BuyItKwik.com

CHAPTER SIX

LONG-TERM WEALTH THROUGH RENTAL PROPERTIES

I was unemployed when I started working with real estate in late 2003. It took me just about three years to go from having a pile of debt to creating a seven-figure positive net worth from building a rental portfolio - something I never thought would happen to me. Since then, I have accelerated my business model and have learned from both my mistakes and from others in the field.

Education is very important in this industry, just like in any other profession. Remember that you have your money on the line. Make it work in your favor. Experience is a great teacher; however, in real estate, education is usually cheaper.

HOW I BECAME A LANDLORD

When I decided to start working with real estate, I really didn't know where to begin. I didn't have a job and my unemployment benefits had run out. I needed money and

I needed it fast, so I began by wholesaling houses to other investors. I needed quick cash, and this worked very well. It was undoubtedly the easiest money I have ever made. After selling around 25 homes over the summer, I started holding a few houses so I could make a return on my investments. I could not pass up the return that I saw some new investor friends getting, and on some of the deals, I was selling to them.

I became a landlord. Now, I had no real knowledge about rentals or land lording when I started. One thing I learned pretty quickly is that one needs patience to be a landlord. I would recommend using a reputable property management company. Be prepared to pay them well for their services.

If you plan to manage your own properties, you should be very familiar with the landlord-tenant laws in your state. I also recommend only buying rental property close to where you live, because you don't want to have to drive all over to check on properties.

FINDING THE RIGHT RENTAL PROPERTY

Finding a great deal is easy once you have identified your target property. You need to do research and develop a plan. Locate rental areas in your city, and find out what these homes rent for. Then, you can work the numbers backwards to see what your maximum investment should be in order to get the return you need. When you figure this out, stick to it. The more you spend above this target price, the less cash flow you will have.

Quick example: In the Oklahoma City metro area, an 1,100-square-foot home with three bedrooms, one and a half

baths, and a one-car garage will rent for $650 to $750 per month. I will pay up to $40,000 for a home like this in good repair, which means that I have to spend less than $1,000 in repairs to make it ready to rent by Section 8 standards.

I recommend that you look for homes that are in the medium rent range to start, such as two- to four-bedroom homes that are less than 40 years old. There will always be demand for these houses. Be creative with financing. You don't have to mortgage each one through a bank, although some of mine are. I don't want mortgage payments that exceed half of the rent. There are a few exceptions to this rule, which vary depending on the property. I don't want a big expense in case the home becomes vacant.

I have yet to find a home that has better cash flow than the very first rental home that I purchased in 2004. I purchased a large split-level home for $53,500, and put about $2,000 in it for some paint and carpet. It is a six-bedroom home that rents for $1,100 per month with a housing-assistance tenant. They are still in the home to this day because they have such a large family. My current payment is $428, and that includes taxes and insurance. That is a positive cash flow of $672 per month on one house.

Be careful not to confuse every great deal that generates equity with a property that would increase your cash flow. It is important to know what the bottom line is on every deal that you work so you know what your exit strategy needs to be.

If you find a home with lots of equity, but it still won't increase your cash flow, then think creatively to make some money. It is probably a great deal to a retail flipper. Sell them your contract for a nice quick profit. Let them repair it and

sell retail on the market. You don't have lift a hammer or a paint brush. Simply sign some contracts and get a check.

In some cases, you can make $10,000 or more from just one deal. This is known as wholesaling. I have also done my fair share of retailing so I could go after the bigger profits.

BUILDING A REMODELING TEAM

Once you have a property, chances are it will need some work, since you paid below retail. Finding good and affordable long-term help can be hard. Unless you are a handyperson and plan on doing all the painting and repairs yourself, you had better start building your team of professionals: contractors, painters, tile setters, carpet layers, title agents, Realtors®, etc.

Choosing a Realtor is very important. Your Realtor needs to be investor-friendly. Contractors are important, too. It can be helpful to find people that understand your way of communicating. My plumber and main contractor are very proficient in sending e-mails, texting, and faxing invoices. I can text my plumber a work order with an address and my tenant's name and number, and he will call the tenant to make the appointment. He faxes me the invoice, and I mail him a check. It doesn't get much easier than that, unless you're a plumber yourself.

Remodeling the homes can cost you a lot if you are not careful. Remember that you are not living in the home, so try not to get personally attached to the condition of it. You need to choose low-cost materials to remodel the homes, but not so cheap that it won't attract tenants.

One thing you can do to simplify this is to use the same white semi gloss paint in all the homes. Don't use custom colors unless you are in a high-end home. If you have to touch up later, you might be hard-pressed to find a paint that is an exact match. Holding onto materials for specific properties for a long time is next to impossible. Use the same carpet, tiles, and doorknobs, for example.

To make the paperwork easier, set up a commercial account at your local home improvement store. Have your contractors pick up supplies. I use a local store that offers a purchase-order-driven system for their accounts receivable customers. When you or your contractor buys something on the account, the cashier asks for a purchase order (P.O.) number. This can simply be the address of the home where the materials will be installed. I get an itemized bill at the end of the month that shows where every penny went. This is great for tracking expenses instead of keeping a bunch of individual receipts, and you can view everything online. I have been using this system for a while and I love it - and so does my accountant.

MAKING YOUR GOALS WORK

For those who want to invest in real estate, I can't stress enough how important it is to set long-term and short-term goals. I plan to own 100 homes by the time I turn 40, at which time I plan to retire from property management and hire a full-time in-house leasing agent who works only for me.

Imagine having the cash flow of 100 homes. What if you sold off a few homes each year to do something you have always wanted to do, like traveling the world, helping out

a loved one, or writing a check to your son's or daughter's college?

I actually found myself in a position to offer temporary housing to the parents of some old military friends who were affected by the hurricanes that hit the Gulf Coast in recent years. At the time, they really didn't know what I was doing for work. They were rather surprised when I called them to offer a vacant house, not to mention very grateful that I would offer this to them. If I hadn't started in this business, I would have never been in a position to help someone out like that.

If you are reserved about diving into real estate full-time, how about part-time? Maybe you don't want to be a landlord. Find buyers of rental property and start wholesaling properties to these landlords. Just open a phone book or look online for homebuyers. This is easy money and there is little risk involved. The biggest investment is a small amount of your spare time spent looking for deals. Trust me, any landlord that seriously wants to buy more rental homes would gladly speak with you about bringing them some good deals. If they don't want to talk with you, then they are simply not smart investors.

I take the time to speak with every wholesaler that I can, mostly because they do the leg work for the deal. I'm willing to pay them for the deal if the numbers work. Last year, I even held a luncheon at a popular restaurant with every wholesaler that I ever purchased a house from. The reason for the luncheon was two-fold. First, I wanted to get them to participate, so I paid for the food. Second, I wanted to know what their goals were for the next year. I also gave out a copy of my goals for the new year. I wanted all of them to know what kind of deals I was looking for and how many I wanted to buy in the coming year. This one lunch resulted

in eight new rentals that those wholesalers brought to me. I didn't have to find the deals. They found me.

Back when I switched over to primarily holding properties as rentals instead of wholesaling, I found that I couldn't find deals quick enough. A woman approached me at our local real estate investing club, and she was interested in making some extra money wholesaling, but she really didn't know how. I could tell that she had the drive and determination to succeed.

Long story short, I showed her what I was looking for and how to find it. She went out and found several potential deals. I went with her and evaluated some of them, and I actually purchased the first one for myself. She went on to contract three other properties, and I helped her find buyers for those because they weren't deals for me. I helped her make over $11,000 in about three months. Some gurus out there would have charged several thousands of dollars for what I did, but I like to be creative. We made an agreement that she would give me first chance at every deal she contracted to buy from then on. I have been able to acquire a few more from her that turned out to be great rentals with some serious equity.

Building long-term relationships with good ethical people is the best way to learn and grow in this business. I am pretty sure that this person will never forget what I simply showed her to do. She took the initiative and went after what she wanted. She made some serious part-time money with no out-of-pocket investment. By the way, she did all this while working a full-time job and being a part-time student.

For more information, check out what Frank Aufiero has to say about wholesaling.

MOVING FORWARD WITHOUT FEAR

If all of this seems overwhelming, take a deep breath. Fear is a natural reaction to what you don't know and aren't familiar with.

DON'T LET FEAR STOP YOU FROM EARNING WHAT YOU ARE WORTH.

Take a look at your current financial situation. Do you think you will be able to retire comfortably enough with the way you *hope* things will play out financially? What would just two or three properties do for you if they are paid off by the time you retire from your full-time job? How about 100 properties?

Do the math and you should see why real estate has made more millionaires than any other profession. Just think - how long would you have to work for someone else to make the same amount of income that you would make if you owned three rental properties - or ten? Imagine owning ten homes free and clear when you retire at $700 each per month in rental income. Isn't it easier to make that money now instead of working hard for someone else over several years to earn it?

People ask me all the time, "How do you do it without making mistakes?" Well, the truth is that I have made many mistakes and have still made money on every deal. Just learn from them and move on. Now, don't take that the wrong way and think that there is no way you can lose money. You can lose everything if you're not careful. Do some research and get educated. Join a local real estate investment group. Log

on to www.nationalreia.com to find one near you. Become a member and get started. Most groups will offer a wealth of knowledge, and they may even offer some affordable classes on different areas of real estate investing.

I have heard dozens of excuses from people as to why they have to wait to start investing. The most popular excuse is that they don't have the money right now or they can't get a loan or they need to clean up their credit. I was unemployed when I started and purchased a very expensive course on a credit card. I began wholesaling to raise funds. Quite simply, the longer you wait to get started, the longer you put off your own retirement.

This is the real deal. You may only experience a downturn in real estate prices once in your lifetime. Right now, in 2009, there is even more of a down market than there was 20 years ago. If you look back five years from now, you will regret not taking action in this down market.

So don't be afraid of getting your feet wet and getting started. That could be your biggest mistake of all. The next few years will be the best time to buy and hold. Take advantage of it. Tomorrow's real estate millionaires are buying real estate today!

JACK L. WERNER, Ph.D., served two tours in Vietnam with the 4ᵗʰ Infantry Division, K Co. 75ᵗʰ Airborne Rangers. After six months in Army hospitals, Jack returned to civilian life and college. After college, he served as an aide to U.S. Congressman Mickey Edwards, spent a quarter of a century with John Hancock, and obtained a Ph.D. in Finance. He now owns A to Z Inspections, one of the largest commercial building and residential inspection companies in Oklahoma. He is also an active real estate investor in the Oklahoma City metro area.

Jack obtained a degree in Construction from OSU and teaches Inspections. OSU/OKC, OGE, Francis Tuttle Technology Center, Moore/Norman Technology Center, and Chickasaw Nation are some of his long-term teaching/training clients. He has served as Commissioner of the OKC Housing Authority, President of the South Oklahoma City Chamber of Commerce, President of the South Oklahoma City Rotary, and President of the State Mental Health Association.

In addition to teaching, writing, performing inspections, and investing in real estate, Jack takes a limited number of clients each year for personal coaching.

Jack Werner can be reached at (405) 412-7861.

CHAPTER SEVEN

HOW NOT TO GET BURNED ON A REAL ESTATE TRANSACTION

Building and Home Inspections for the
Real Estate Investor

BE THERE OR BE SQUARE

The saying from the '60s can apply to one of the most important aspects of a home or building inspection: Do I get the full, final, completed report with dollar cost estimates reviewed with me in detail, on site, at the end of the inspection?

People do not even know that they need to ask this question when booking an inspection. About one-third of the inspection companies do not provide you with a final report on site; you don't get it for two or three days. In my opinion, you lose half the value of your inspection if you do not receive your final copy on site and have a twenty- or thirty-minute detailed explanation and review.

Barry Stone, the national syndicated writer of "Inspector's in the House", agrees. You are wasting your money if you do not get an on-site, walk-around, point-talk-and-explain, final report with dollar cost estimates by your inspector.

You need to clearly ask this question when booking or agreeing to an inspection, and you need to be there at the end of the inspection. Be there or be square!

LEARN ABOUT THE BUILDINGS YOU BUY

Are you becoming a real estate investor? One of the best foundational building blocks is to go on ten inspections.

Learning a great deal more about houses and/or commercial buildings is one of those unique pieces of knowledge that will serve you, your business, and your family in real life use on a regular basis.

- You will be able to gauge if it's pretty, but cheaply built.
- You will know symptoms/signs that may indicate major problems and what type of expert to call for further evaluation.
- You will be able to approximate roof age and life expectancy.
- You will know the most common safety problems.
- You will develop a feel for maintenance items (a few hundred dollars) versus major repairs (thousands of dollars).

In my opinion, by going on five inspections, you will be way ahead of most property buyers and will start to get a handle on where and how to look. If you go on ten

inspections, you'll probably know enough to catch most significant items. Here is how to do it:

- Purchase one inspection from the inspection company that has the reputation of being the most thorough.

- Only purchase from an inspection company which has that reputation and that agrees to take you, at no charge, on additional inspections. A to Z Inspections works in Central Oklahoma and trains inspectors. We have always welcomed students and trainees. Two inspectors attend every inspection, and trainees are limited to two per inspection. If you can make it to Oklahoma City, you may go on inspections at no charge. Just call (405) 412-7861.

- Ask for and get a blank copy of the inspection form used by your inspector so that you can make copies and use it as a checklist yourself on future inspections that you attend and on future properties that you purchase.

- If you are not willing to attend a minimum of five inspections, in my opinion, you are wasting your time and placing yourself in financial danger because you are too impatient. I encourage you to go on ten inspections. The real quantum leap in understanding won't happen before that. I require that anyone working with A to Z attend 25 inspections and participate in 70 hours of classroom training.

QUESTIONS FOR THE INSPECTOR

What you are after is the most thorough inspection available by highly competent inspectors and an opportunity

for you to learn. How do you secure the most thorough inspection? Ask these seven questions:

- "Will I receive my final detailed report with dollar cost estimates in detail with me at the end of the inspection?"
- "Approximately how many man-hours will I get on my inspection?"
- "Has every inspector in your company passed the National Home Inspection Exam?"
- "What experience or certifications would you like to tell me about?"
- "With which national organization are you affiliated?"
- "If I need _____, will you arrange for it and/or perform the inspection?"
  a. Water Well Inspection
  b. Septic Tank Inspection
  c. Swimming Pool Inspection
  d. Termite Inspection
  e. Structural Inspection
  f. Duct Scoping
- "May we go on inspections with you?"

If you are a real estate investor or wish to become a real estate investor, you are an entrepreneur at heart and that means you need to be patient.